POCKET BUILDER
NATURE

Let's get building!

WRITTEN BY
TORI KOSARA

INTRODUCTION

This book is packed with ideas and tricks to help you become a better LEGO® builder, whether you're building with LEGO bricks for the first or the thousandth time. Start with the handy building tips on page 4, and then grab your LEGO collection, choose a page, and go wild! With advice and building techniques for making animals, plants, and natural wonders, you'll be a LEGO building expert in no time. What will you make?

Find me on page 24!

Where should I start?

Dive in for building fun!

BUILDING TIPS

Are you ready to start thinking like a LEGO builder? Try some of these ideas, or come up with your own way of doing things. The most important thing to remember is to have fun!

GETTING STARTED

There's one thing you'll definitely need before you can build: LEGO pieces! Don't worry about the size of your collection or how new it is. The original LEGO® System in Play elements (made from 1958) fit perfectly with those made today. You can also buy second-hand LEGO pieces at thrift stores, share with friends and neighbors, or play with them at schools and libraries.

What size will your model be?

SCALE UP OR DOWN

Decide what scale you want your model to be before you start so that you have the right number of LEGO pieces ready.

SORT YOUR BRICKS

Organize your collection into element types and colors to save time as you build.

4

FIND A BUILDING SPACE

Look for a flat surface with plenty of room for building and storing your pieces, such as a table.

SWAP IT OUT

If you don't have the perfect piece, think about other parts you can use instead.

BUILD TOGETHER

Ask a family member or a friend to join in and share the joy of building. You might learn new things from each other!

Who wants to build with me?

CHOOSE YOUR COLORS

Use whatever colors you like when you're building. Your models can look however you want!

I would look great in pink!

DON'T PANIC!

There is no right or wrong way to build. If your model doesn't turn out how you wanted it to, rebuild it or try something new.

KEEP BUILDING

The fun is in the building, so just keep connecting your bricks until things click for you.

CHAPTER 1
ANIMAL LIFE

TOOTHY SHARK

These underwater predators need to move quickly along the reef to hunt for tasty fish. Use angular shapes like slopes and flag pieces for streamlined fins that let your shark swim swiftly.

What a fin-tastic build!

Stack of two slope bricks creates an iconic dorsal fin

2×2 trapezoid flag can move up and down on the bar it's clipped to

1×1 double slope for a pointy lower jaw

LOOK SHARP

Reef sharks have large teeth on the top and narrow chompers on the bottom. Use a variety of plates with teeth for a sharp look.

1×1 plate with tooth

1×2 plate with teeth

PETITE PENGUIN

Antarctic-dwelling Adélie penguins can spend hours swimming through icy waters. But on land, they are often standing on two webbed feet—some even sleep this way. Keep your penguin steady with a small baseplate.

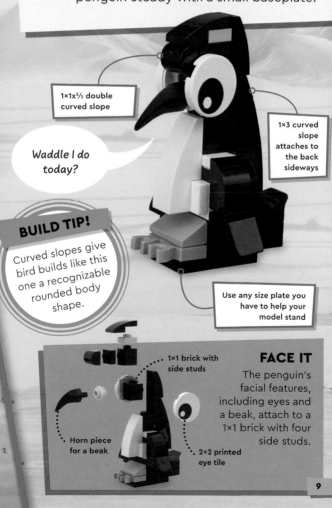

1×1x²⁄₃ double curved slope

1×3 curved slope attaches to the back sideways

Waddle I do today?

BUILD TIP!

Curved slopes give bird builds like this one a recognizable rounded body shape.

Use any size plate you have to help your model stand

1×1 brick with side studs

FACE IT

The penguin's facial features, including eyes and a beak, attach to a 1×1 brick with four side studs.

Horn piece for a beak

2×2 printed eye tile

MICRO MANATEE

Make small but mighty creatures with just a handful of pieces! This microbuild is made mainly by stacking small gray plates. Two slopes add shape and make it easy to identify this "sea cow."

BUILD TIP!

Think carefully about the shape of your model and look for pieces to help you achieve it.

4×1 double curved slope shapes the manatee's back

Real manatees are enormous!

Add features such as a tail and flippers

1×1×1 ²/₃ slope with plate makes the head

MINI FLIPPERS

The tiny flippers are 1×1 tiles that slot into 1×1 plates with clips. The tail is built in the same way.

1×1 plate with clip

1×1 tile

SMALL SQUIRREL

The core of the tiny squirrel's body is made from just two small bricks— a 1×1 brick with side studs stacked on a 1×1 headlight brick. Both pieces let you connect small parts all around so you can add all of the critter's features.

The tail is a sideways stack of plates and one curved slope

I'm made of just 12 pieces!

Two 1×1 plates with clips make hands perfect for grabbing branches

1×1 headlight brick for the bottom of the body

1×1 tile with clip

1×1 brick with side studs

1×1 plate with clip for feet

ALL EARS

Get creative with your pieces. Just one small piece makes both the top of the model's head and the two ears!

PRETTY PEACOCK

Male peafowl, called peacocks, are known for showing off their beautiful trains. Recreate eye-catching tail feathers by decorating a large curved plate with magnificently colored 1×1 round plates.

Plates with teeth create feathered edges

I'm a fan of this look!

1×3×2 curved arch for a birdlike neck

This curved slope looks like a folded wing

BUILD TIP!

Think about the colors you need and set them aside before you start to build.

FAN ON

To achieve a realistic angle, attach the peacock's fan of tail feathers to a hinge plate and hinge brick.

4×8 curved plate

2×2 hinge plate

IMPRESSIVE EAGLE

Eagles have an impressive wingspan! To help your eagle model soar through the skies, you can use long wedge plates to create wings or connect smaller wedge plates on top of standard plates until the wings are the right length.

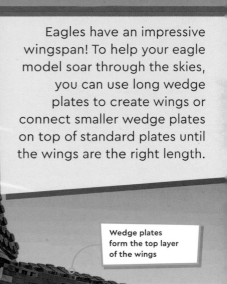

Wedge plates form the top layer of the wings

Wing it with the pieces you have!

1×2 plate with teeth makes convincing talons

UP AND DOWN

Ball and socket joint connections let this model's wings "flap" and bend for a more realistic look.

1×2 plate with ball joint

1×2 plate with socket

HAPPY HIPPO

A hippopotamus's large, rounded body has smooth, sensitive skin. Use slopes to shape the body and be sure to cover up any studs to give your hippo model's "skin" a sleek look.

BUILD TIP!

Look at pictures of real-life animals to help you make your models look more realistic.

1×2 plate with bar ....

OPEN WIDE

A plate with bar on the hippo's head fits into pieces with clips so its powerful jaw can open and shut.

Clip .....

Snap to it!

Three 2×4 double curved slopes form the top of the hippo's back

Join 2×2×2 round bricks and 2×2 round plates for legs

CAMO CHAMELEON

Chameleons are masters of camouflage because they can change the color of their skin to blend in with their surroundings. Try building your lizard's body in one color scheme and then rebuild it in another!

> I shouldn't have tried that tongue twister.

3×2×1 slope creates a curved body

2×2 domes make feet fit for climbing trees

Curved arches for a bendy tail that wraps around branches

LICKETY-SPLIT

1×2 jumper plate

Lasso

Adding a tongue is quick work. A lasso piece fits into a 1×2 jumper plate, which attaches to the head sideways.

LIVELY LOBSTER

Dive into your LEGO® collection and search for curved slope pieces to build a lifelike lobster like this one. Different sizes and types of curved pieces form the claws and the shell-like body of this model.

> Let's make it snappy!

2×2 curved slope shapes the lobster's back

Antennules attach to the lobster's head, which is a 2×2 double curved slope

BUILD TIP!

Lobsters have large pincers, so be sure to use your longest curved slopes to make the claws.

Two curved slopes make the claw

LITTLE LEGS

Four 1×1 plates with clips fit onto the underside of the lobster's body to make tiny lobster legs.

1×1 plate with clip

1×1 double curved slope

AMAZING ANGELFISH

Almost all of this eye-catching tropical fish model is built by stacking bricks and plates on their sides. Make sure the face of the fish is narrower than the rest of the body to get the right shape.

Printed eye tile fits onto a 1×1 brick with side studs

The tail pieces are stacked sideways in the opposite direction of the rest of the model

I'm ready to make a splash!

TOP TO BOTTOM

The fins are the only part of the fish that are not built sideways. They are made of a stack of two plates, a curved slope, and a tile.

4×1 curved slope

Tile

WONDERFUL WHALE

Large sea creatures don't have to be ocean-sized! Scale down your models to make sure you have enough pieces to build your creations. You could even try to make a whale with just a few bricks.

The stud on this jumper plate makes a blowhole

I'm having a whale of a time!

Eyes attach to headlight bricks on either side of the whale's head

BUILD TIP!

Build the core of the whale's body first and then add the slopes, head, and tail.

Different curved pieces give the whale its shape

Two curved slopes fit onto a bracket plate to make the tail

STUCK IN THE MIDDLE

Bracket plates line the edges of the inside of the whale's body so that curved slopes can attach to its tops and sides.

1×2/2×2 bracket plate

1×1 headlight brick

Curved slope

POOPING PARROT

This jungle bird has a surprise-wing move! Inside its "tummy" are two gears that turn when the wing is pulled forward. Fill the space covered by the tail with brown 1×1 round bricks.

Beak is a small slope attached to a plate with clip

Two LEGO® Technic gears are hidden under these pieces

Lift my left wing to turn the gears.

•••••• **Tail moves up and down on two pin connectors**

•••••• **1×1 round brick**

TAIL FEATHERS

The two gears knock into a LEGO Technic connector that forces the trapdoor tail to open so that the parrot's "poop" pops out.

Tan plates with teeth look like clawed feet

BUILD TIP!

Don't worry if you don't have these pieces. You can build a parrot with what you do have!

ACROBATIC ANACONDA

Make a bendy anaconda by using plates with ball and socket joints. You can make the snake's body as long as you like and change the shape as you play. You can also use click hinges if you don't have enough ball and socket pieces.

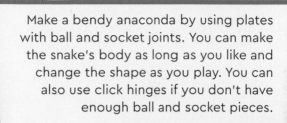

Make scales using 1×2 plates in any colors you like

1×2 plate with socket joint

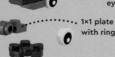

Sss-pectacular building!

Use a 1×2 plate with ball joint at the end for the tail

1×1 printed eye tile

1×1 plate with ring

SNAKE EYES

The snake's printed tile eyes attach sideways to two 1×1 plates with rings.

SOARING PTERANODON

All you need is a handful of LEGO bricks to transport you back in time. Grab yours and build an ancient reptile like this pteranodon (teh-ran-oh-don). No one knows what color they were, so go wild!

I look pter-iffic!

Dagger pieces for streamlined feet

Toothless beak is made from a large claw piece

Tiles help hold together various sizes of plates

BUILD TIP!

Build the pteranodon's wings symmetrically so they are the same on both sides.

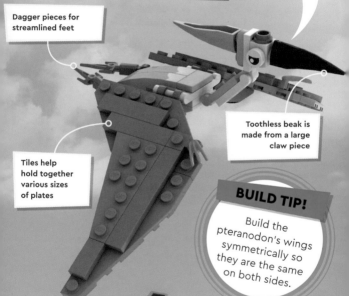

8×3 wedge plate

1×2 plate with clips

UNDER WING

1×2 plates with clips on the underside of each wing connect to the plates with bars in the body.

ROVING T-REX

Strike a pose! There are lots of flexible connections in this T-rex model, so its legs, arms, head, jaw, and tail can be moved. This way you can change the T-rex's position as you play or when creating a fierce dinosaur display.

Neck moves on a ball and socket joint connection

Ball and socket connections along the tail make it flexible

Let's get moving!

Plate with click hinge

LEG IT

Click hinges let the lower legs move back and forth so that the T-rex model can "walk."

MASSIVE MAMMOTH

Building prehistoric creatures isn't a mammoth task! This woolly mammoth is built in sections. Build the torso, head, and legs separately and then join them together. Add the tusks and trunk last.

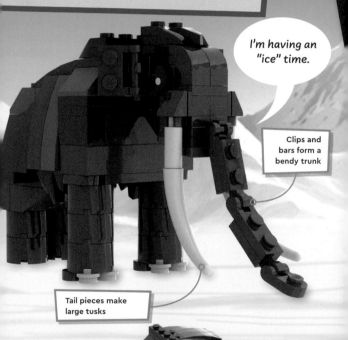

I'm having an "ice" time.

Clips and bars form a bendy trunk

Tail pieces make large tusks

STURDY LEGS

Stacks of 2×2 round bricks make strong legs to support the mammoth's large body.

Back legs are one brick shorter

Four 1×1 round plates form foot pads

2×2 round brick

EXCELLENT ELEPHANT

The torso of this woolly mammoth's modern-day relative is made up of stacks of standard bricks and plates. Attach curved slopes to the underside to make a realistic rounded tummy.

You could use tiles instead of plates for a smoother look

Building is elephantastic fun!

This piece is usually used to make cattle horns

Upside-down slopes form solid legs

1×2 jumper plate

1×3×2 curved arch

FRONT AND CENTER

Two jumper plates keep the trunk lined up in the middle of the elephant's face.

BUILD TIP!

Be sure to build bricks with side studs into the head if you want to add eyes.

SPOTTED GIRAFFE

Reach new heights with a giraffe build like this one! A hinge brick and plate hold the long neck at an angle. If you don't have hinge pieces, connect the base of the neck to a standard brick instead.

It won't take long to build me!

Stack up bricks to make the neck

BUILD TIP!

Make sure the neck isn't so tall that it causes your model to topple over!

Hinge bricks are at the top and bottom of the neck

Pieces in different shades of brown make a patterned coat

2×2 curved slope

1×2 white plate for teeth

Inverted curved slope

SMILE!
Plates sandwiched between curved slopes on the top and bottom of the mouth form the shape of the muzzle.

CHEEKY CHIMP

This little chimpanzee has plenty of character even though it's made from just a handful of pieces. Sideways connections let you add lots of features to make a charming little ape!

1×1 slope "ears" connect to bricks with side studs

Don't hang around—get building!

2×2 corner plate looks like a bendy arm

2×2 round tile "tummy" fits onto bricks with side studs

SURPRISING DETAIL

The hole in this 1×2 jumper plate makes a convincing chimp mouth when connected to a bracket plate.

1×2/2×2 bracket plate

1×2 jumper plate

LUCKY LADYBUG

Some people believe that ladybugs are lucky. Build a little ladybug lucky charm and make your own luck! Use red plates to form the insect's body. Attach as many small black round tiles as you like to form the ladybug's spots.

Stack plates to make the ladybug's shell look curved at the top

I'm feeling lucky!

1×1 round plates with bars make adorable antennae

Battle droid arms clip to a plate with octagonal bars to form legs

4×4 plate

1×1 brick with side studs

ALL FOUR IT

1×1 bricks with side studs placed at each corner of the body let you attach the ladybug's shell on all four sides and on the top, too.

BUILD TIP!

Use any thin pieces with clips you have in your collection to create spindly insect legs.

BUSY BUMBLEBEE

Wouldn't it "bee" great to build a larger-than-life minibeast like this one? Grab your bricks and make a model of an insect at any scale you like. This bumblebee is just a bit larger than the real thing, but yours could be huge or tiny.

I am buzzing with excitement!

Stacks of 2×2 round plates in alternating colors make stripes

2×1 wedge slopes form the bee's long face

Six robot arms with clips attach to upside-down plates with bars

2×2 inverted round plate

1×2 round plate

BUZZ OFF

Two transparent 2×2 inverted round plates fit into two 1×2 round plates at the top of the thorax (body) to make it look as though the bee is ready to take flight.

JUMPY JACKRABBIT

Jackrabbits are quick critters. They can reach speeds of 40 mph (64 kph)—that's as fast as a high-speed electric scooter! Curved slopes built into the model's back make it look as though the jackrabbit is poised to leap off at top speed.

Curved slope ears attach to bricks with side studs

Did you know I'm a hare, not a rabbit?

BUILD TIP!

Study your creature's features and find the perfect piece. For example, jackrabbits have long ears.

1×1 plate secured to a jumper plate looks like a nose

2×1×1 ⅓ curved slopes for legs that are ready to hop!

HARE CLIP

A bar at the base of the model's head fits onto a 1×2 tile with clip on the body so that it can move up and down.

Head connects to the plates below ....

.... **1×2 tile with clip**

CLEVER RAT

This rat's body is shaped by many different types of slope bricks. Slopes of various sizes are stacked to make the legs, ears, face, and the back of the body. Look through your collection to find out what sizes of slopes you have before you build.

Joysticks form the rat's tail and whiskers

Glowing eyes are red light-bulb pieces with bars

1×1 slopes are also sometimes called "cheese slopes"

Did someone say cheese?

ABOUT FACE

The pieces that form the rat's sniffy snout attach to all sides of a 1×1 brick with side studs.

1×1 brick with side studs

1×1 round plate with petals

Some bunny's been eating my veggies.

CHAPTER 2
PLANT LIFE

WONDROUS WATER LILY

You don't need a giant LEGO® collection to create a magnificent water lily like this one. This model's circular base is built on four round corner plates, but you can also use half circle plates.

That looks like a nice place to catch flies!

Use 1×1 round plates with petals to add flowers

4×4 round corner plate forms part of the base

Leave open studs in the center for LEGO wildlife to sit on

GO IN CIRCLES

Curved slope pieces attach sideways to bracket plates on four sides of the lily pad to form a circular shape around its edges.

1×2/1×2 bracket plate

3×1 curved slope

REMARKABLE RHODODENDRON

Bring a piece of a tree-sized plant into your home by building flowers and leaves from a forest-dwelling rhododendron. You can add as many green leaves as you like by attaching them to the flowers using plate and clip connections.

Flower stem piece looks like the stamen and pollen

Use curved slopes to make a rounded leaf shape

1×2 curved slopes make perfect petals

1×1 plate with bar

1×1 brick with side studs

SURROUNDED

One 1×1 brick with side studs holds each flower and the plates with bars onto which the leaves clip.

BUILD TIP!

Build the flowers one by one before attaching them to the center of the plant.

PLEASANT PINE TREES

Create a whole outdoor scene with just a couple of models such as these pine trees. Each layer of branches is made of small slopes stacked on a plate. Build little snowbanks to complete the frosty look.

> Stack slopes at angles to make the pine trees' branches

Who put that tree there?

> Create snow-covered branches with small white pieces

> Snowy base of white pieces keeps the trees steady

SKI JUMP

Use a jumper plate to support the top layer of branches and keep them centered in the pine tree.

2×2 jumper plate

2×2 round brick trunk

FANTASTIC FOREST

To make each tree for this forest, simply stack up brown 2×2 bricks to form the trunk. Top the trunk with half arch pieces to make bendy branches to which the leaves can be attached. Make trees of different sizes to build a whole forest.

Change the color of the leaves with the seasons

Add more plant pieces to the forest floor

Stack of six 2×2 brown bricks makes the trunk

BUILD TIP!

This tree is top-heavy. It needs to be attached to a baseplate to stop it from tipping over.

Let's hop to it!

10×10 octagonal plate for a grassy base

6×5 plant leaf fits onto a plate with hooks

LEAFY LAYERS

The leaf pieces slide onto each of the four hooks of the 2×2 round plate with hooks to form the topmost layer.

ELEGANT ORCHID

If you can't spot any of these precious plants in the wild, build one instead! The colorful petals on this model are 3×3 round corner plates. They attach to a stem made of green 1×1 round bricks.

Small quarter circle tiles add definition to the petals

I've finally found the rarest orchid!

BUILD TIP!

Add a 2×2 round jumper plate at the bottom of the stem for extra stability.

Center the 1×1 round plate "pollen" on a jumper plate

Vine pieces slot into 1×1 round plates with holes for leaves

SET THE BAR

The top petal fits onto a 1×1 round plate with bar that slides into a 1×1 brick with side studs at the top of the stem.

1×1 round plate with bar

1×1 brick with side studs

COOL CACTUS

The center stem of this desert-dwelling cactus is made entirely from one type of brick! Stack up green 2×4 bricks in a crisscross pattern until your cactus is as tall as you want it to be.

I hope I don't get stuck!

Tall stack of 2×4 bricks

Tan 16×16 plate supports the cactus

Add a frame of plates in the shape of a cross to help you stack up your bricks

ARMS OUT

2×4 bricks are stacked outward

1×3 inverted slope shapes the arm

To add arms, build outward before you stack the next level on top. Use curved pieces for a bendy look.

CHARMING PLANT

Create a ring of petals for a potted plant like this one by clipping colorful pieces to a round plate with octagonal bars. Your cheerful LEGO® plant will look bright all year round—no watering needed!

Pollen is a 2×2 dome stuck to the center of the plate with octagonal bars

Change the color of the slopes throughout the year

Leaf fits onto a plate with bar that attaches to the stem

Isn't this blooming marvelous?

POTTER AROUND

The inner core of the pot is made by stacking 1×4 bricks with side studs. Attach curved slopes on all four sides of the block for a rounded shape.

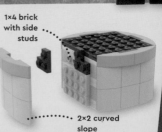

1×4 brick with side studs

2×2 curved slope

TERRIFIC TREES

Palm trees are found in many tropical climates. Build a lush forest filled with palms for your minifigures to enjoy. 6×5 swordleaf pieces easily slide onto plates with hooks that sit atop the trees' trunks.

BUILD TIP!

Connect green plates to make the forest floor as big or as small as you want.

Add 1×1 round plates with petals to look like ripe fruit

Green curved slope creates a mossy jungle floor

JUMP UP

A 2×2 jumper plate keeps the 1×1×6 pillar tree trunk centered. Attach trunks made from round or standard bricks to standard plates.

1×1×6 pillar

2×2 jumper plate

ENCHANTING RAIN FOREST

A rain forest teems with plant and wildlife from the dark, damp forest floor to the bright, windswept canopy. Use your LEGO bricks to build leafy trees. Then add plenty of plants and animals to your forest.

2×2 ridged round bricks make sturdy tree trunks

1×1 truncated cones look like mushroom tops

Gather all your plant pieces and green bricks before you start building.

LEGO® Technic half pin

1×1 tile with clip

Bar with handle

IN THE SWING

The bar "branch" fits into a tile with clip. It can move up and down on a LEGO Technic pin.

Whee—this is so fun!

It's easy to add flowers with 1×1 round plates with petals

Two 1×1 round plates with plant leaves make the perfect home for minibeasts

43

MIGHTY MONKEY PUZZLE

The branches on these trees grow at so many angles, they might even puzzle a climbing monkey! Attach round bricks to bricks with side studs so your branches can grow in different directions.

BUILD TIP!

Make the bottom branches the longest so the shape gets narrower as you build up.

Most of the leaves are green 1×1 round bricks

2×2 ridged round bricks form a tree trunk with bark

1×1 brick with side studs

BRANCH OUT

Bar pieces make the base of the large branches. They fit into 1×1 bricks with side studs that form part of the tree's trunk.

Slide leaf pieces onto the bars

STUNNING ROOF GARDEN

You can find nature in unexpected places—even in big cities! Top your LEGO homes and flats with flourishing plants and flowers so your minifigure residents have plenty of green space to relax in.

Vine pieces connect to a 1×1 brick with side studs

Inverted dome holds this potted plant in place

Let's grow upstairs!

Plant stems hold these flower pieces

Leaves clip onto plates with bars

GET GROWING

Stick together all the plant and flower pieces you have to create lots of interesting plants for your roof garden.

CHEERFUL CHERRY TREE

Make a serene scene where artistic minifigures can get inspiration for their creative pursuits. Stack slopes and arches at angles to create a tall cherry tree for your minifigures to rest beneath as they daydream.

Build in half arches to create bendy branches

Build trees on top of plates to keep them steady

Nature is so inspiring!

Leaf elements can be any colors you have in your collection

Small flower

PINNED IN

The pins on the flower elements slot into the open studs in the leaf elements to form cherry blossoms.

Add lanterns by topping 1×1 headlight bricks with radar dishes

GREAT GRASS

Make a cozy hiding place for your minibeast builds and small creature models such as birds by building tall grasses. Different-colored bars with stoppers are perfect for creating tall blades of grass.

That looks like a nice place to rest!

Flower stems make short, spiky blades of grass

BUILD TIP!

Vary the heights of the blades of grass by slotting the bars into different types of pieces with holes.

Cover the studs of sandy-colored plates with "grass"

NO HOLES BARRED

Each bar with stopper is held in place by a 1×1 round plate with hole or a 1×1 cone.

Bar with stopper ·········

1×1 round plate with hole ·········

PERFECT PUMPKIN PATCH

Pick plenty of orange plates from your collection so that you can build a great gourd like this plump pumpkin. Build pumpkins in various sizes and even different colors. Then set up a prize-winning pumpkin patch for your minifigures to visit.

Layer small orange plates to make a rounded shape

Building this is as easy as pie!

Connect large leaf elements to any studs on the model

1×1 brick with side studs

Stack of orange plates

INSIDE SCOOP

Orange plates connect to two frames made of 1×4 and 1×1 bricks with side studs that are inside the pumpkin.

BRIGHT GARDEN

Botanical gardens are filled with eye-catching plants and flowers from all over the world. Use a variety of pieces in different sizes, shapes, and colors to "grow" your own brick-built botanicals.

Golden stem looks like this flower's pistil

Stack up different leaf pieces to give plants height

Add a fence or a wall to the garden if you like

PLATE UP

The base of the garden is made up of plates. Build your plants and then attach them to the plates to create a lush garden.

Curly plant stem

1×1 round plate with petals ....

8×8 half circle plate ....

I've picked my favorite!

Upside-down cone pieces make colorful petals

CUTE CLOVER

Make your own luck by building a four-leaf clover. You'll need four heart plates to form the leaves. You can magically transform it into a flower by swapping out the green for colorful heart plates instead!

Heart plate attaches to a 2×4 plate underneath

I've finally found a four-leaf clover!

The clover is built on top of this narrow plate

MAGICAL SECRET

The secret to this build is three 1×2 jumper plates. The pieces fit onto the stem and center the 2×4 plate that the leaves attach to.

1×2 jumper plate · · · · · · · · ·

BEAUTIFUL CROCUS

If you don't have a green thumb, build a garden of life-size flowers with your LEGO bricks instead. Crocuses are one of the first flowers to pop up in early spring in many places, so why not get started with one of these?

Four joysticks look like the flower's stamens

Four 4×2 curved slopes form the petals

Use any size or shape plate you like as the base

1×2/2×2 bracket plate

Stack of 1×1 round bricks for the stem

IN BLOOM

The curved slope petals attach to 1×2/2×2 brackets, which also form the center of the flower.

Nature is such a treasure!

CHAPTER 3
NATURAL WONDERS

RUGGED VOLCANO

Build an active volcano for your minifigures to watch—from a safe distance, of course! To make a rocky mountain like this one, stack up lots of different sizes of gray slope bricks.

White ice cream scoops look like billowing smoke

Transparent red, yellow, and orange pieces for lava

Make the base of the volcano wider than the top

Build the volcano on a large baseplate like this

FLOW DOWN

A 1×2 plate with two bars fits into a plate with clip in the volcano so the lava flow can be angled downward.

1×2 plate with two bars

Plate with clip

FANTASTIC FERN FOSSIL

No luck digging for fossils? Study some pictures of the real thing and then build your own. This fern is made by stacking up gray 1×1 round bricks and 1×1 plates with bars to form the stony stem. Each leaf clips onto one of the bars.

What an incredible discovery!

BUILD TIP!

Fossils tend to be colored like rocks and stones, so use gray, black, and tan pieces.

1×1 plate with bar connects the leaf to the stem

Stack of black bricks makes a rock-like background

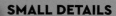

.... 1×2 plate

.... 1×2 curved slope leaf

SMALL DETAILS

Ferns have curved leaves. Add small curved slope pieces on top of plates to get the shape.

FROSTY WOODLAND

This cool winter scene is built entirely from white pieces to make it look like everything in the forest is covered in a layer of freshly fallen snow. You could add other wintry colors, too, such as transparent blue pieces for ice.

Challenge friends to spot camouflaged creatures

Stack white slopes at angles for branches

I should have checked the weather . . .

Curved slopes form snowdrifts

SNOWY STEM

The pins on horn pieces fit into 1×2 jumper plates to look like snow-covered shoots in the woods.

Horn piece

1×2 jumper plate

SWEET SPRING FOREST

BUILD TIP!

A double layer of baseplates makes your build extra sturdy so it can be moved easily.

In some parts of the world, spring is the time for plants to grow and minifigures to head outdoors as snow melts. Change your wintry scene to a spring one by using different-colored bricks.

Pines stay green throughout the seasons

Oh dear!

Transparent pieces look like melting ice

1×1 plate with clip

1×3 plate

Slope for the head

SPRING AHEAD

Add wildlife to the scene, such as a darling deer. Make antlers by stacking up 1×1 plates at angles on top of a 1×3 plate.

MAGNIFICENT MOUNTAINS

It won't take a mountain of bricks to build these rocky hills. Start with a long line of gray bricks and stack upward, making sure that the bottom of the build is the widest part of the triangular shape. Use white pieces to add a snowy landscape.

Stack up white bricks at the top for snowy peaks

I want to catch another fish!

Use gray slopes to form steep mountainsides

Two sideways arches form a hole in the ice

SNOWCAPS

Build a few white plates into the stony gray mountain to make the polar peaks look more realistic.

Small slope

2×8 plate

PERILOUS QUICKSAND

Minifigures need to watch their step! The tan plates and bricks might look like dusty dirt, but it's really sticky quicksand. This model also has a hidden trapdoor that reveals a pit when the lever is pulled.

BUILD TIP!

Leave the hole uncovered if you don't want a trapdoor in your model.

I'm just out for a quick walk...

Pull this handle to activate the trap

These two small tan plates aren't connected

1×4 brick for a quicksand pit border

Tile acts as a stopper

Tiles stop the slider from sticking to the base

2×6 plate

IT'S A TRAP!

Pulling the handle on the slider causes the two loose plates to fall into the pit—along with any passersby!

FROTHY OCEAN SURF

You can build a whole ocean scene on just one large baseplate! Build wild waves onto a blue plate like this one. Then let your minifigures ride the surf or display your art on a shelf.

Surf's up!

1×2 grille tiles look like frothy sea foam

Curvy macaroni bricks make great ocean waves

Attach creatures such as fish to plates with clips

THAT'S SWELL

The macaroni bricks are the tallest pieces on this model. They create waves that look like a high ocean swell.

Plates for flat surf

1×1 round plate is just shorter than the brick

DAZZLING SUN

With lots of small orange and yellow pieces, you can build a mosaic of the sun to brighten up the grayest days. Use transparent and gold pieces for extra shine.

BUILD TIP!

If you don't have large plates, you can build your mosaic on smaller plates and join them together.

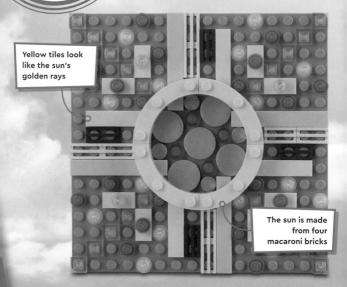

Yellow tiles look like the sun's golden rays

The sun is made from four macaroni bricks

1×1 round plate

BRIGHT IDEA

Use 1×1 transparent orange tiles and 1×1 round plates so that rays stretch out from the sun diagonally.

1×1 transparent tile

63

RADIANT RAINBOW

Brighten up every day with a rainbow! Stack bricks and plates like a staircase on top of plates to keep your rainbow upright. You can use the classic colors or make any pattern you like.

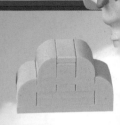

Connect both sides of the rainbow with plates

Most of the rainbow is built with 1×2 bricks

HEAD IN THE CLOUDS

Build puffy clouds to add to your build. Curved slopes like these form the rounded sides.

.... 1×4×1 ⅓ curved slope

BUILD TIP!

Start with the bottom layer of the rainbow and stack pieces upward in an arch shape.

Use one large baseplate or a few smaller plates instead

SUNNY SUMMER DAY

Try making one model and transform it to match the seasons as they change! This summery tree house sits on a lush green plate that's just right for spreading out a brick-built picnic blanket.

Dark green leaves could be replaced with lighter shades for spring

Lemonade, please!

Keep the brown tree trunk the same throughout the year

1×1 plates and tiles form a checked blanket

TREE ANGLE

1×2 hinge bricks and 2×2 hinge plates on either side of the tree house hold the sloping sides at an angle.

1×1 slopes for roof tiles

1×2 hinge brick

CRISP FALL EVENING

If there's a chill in the air, it's time to swap out summery colors for the browns, yellows, oranges, and golds of fall. Just a few small changes make a big difference!

BUILD TIP!

Find pieces in your collection that match the colors of the season where you live.

Even the wildlife changes with the seasons

Tan base looks like a leaf-covered yard

Where did I leave my rake?

7×3 ladder with clips

CLIP AND CLIMB

The end of the bottom ladder fits into the clips of the one above it. Thanks to the clip and bar connection, it can flip up and down.

CRAGGY CANYON

A canyon is a deep valley with tall, rocky sides. This model gets its height from two tan-colored rock panel pieces. If you don't have rock panels, use tall bricks or stack up smaller elements instead.

BUILD TIP!

Place the two large rock panels on your base before you add slopes and plants.

Two 4×10×6 rock panels form the base on either side of a cave

Stack wedge plates on the base to create rocky terrain

Swap the tan plate for blue if you want a river running through your canyon

SLIPPERY SLOPES

Canyons are known for steep sides, so be sure to use lots of different slope bricks on your model.

2×4 slope brick

BIG BOULDERS

Boulders are large rocks. Usually they are worn down by wind or rain and that makes them smooth. Slope pieces have large areas without studs, so they work well as the weathered sides of boulders.

This is not the kind of rock I was expecting!

Leave some studs exposed for a rougher texture

2×4 slope brick forms a sharp, angular end

6×4 triple curved wedge makes a smooth side

Green piece looks like moss

4×4 inverted triple curved wedge

WEDGED IN

Wedge pieces form the bases of both of these boulders and give the models their rounded shape.

INCREDIBLE DINO BONES

Want to go on a dinosaur dig? Design your own dino fossils using LEGO® bricks and unearth prehistoric creatures from the comfort of your home. Use white tiles and plates to form the dino's bones.

I have a bone to pick with that dinosaur!

Use macaroni tiles to add curves to the skull

A row of plates with teeth makes the dino's chompers

Tan plates and slopes look like sandstone

FIRST BASE

For this build, you need to make the base and then attach your bone build, such as this dinosaur skull.

Skull pieces are not connected

Plates hold the fossil in place

SPIKY STALACTITES

These rocky spikes are formed over many years as water drips from the roof of a cave. Eventually, minerals in the water harden to form stalactites. Stalagmites form upward. Both models are made from tan bricks and slopes and attach to rocky gray plates.

BUILD TIP!

Build the stalactites by stacking upward on the plate. Then flip the plate upside down.

2×1×3 slope brick is topped with a 1×1 tile

I've got to call someone about that drip . . .

Stack 1×1 bricks at different heights to make stalagmites

1×1 double slope ······

TIP TOP

The stalagmites get their pointy tips from 1×1 double slopes, which are stacked on top of 1×1 bricks.

BUSTLING WILDLIFE POND

Even a small pond can be home to lots of different plants and animals. Use blue plates of any size to make a watery base. Then build plants and animals or use molded pieces to fill your inviting pond habitat.

BUILD TIP!

Try to build your pond on a flat surface with plenty of room, such as a table.

Cattails are 1×1 cones and bars topped with 1×1 round bricks

1×1 round bricks support and add height to plant leaves

Different-sized brown wedge plates make muddy banks

2×2 round bricks form a line of stepping stones

HOME TWEET HOME

Add a birdhouse for those with weary wings to rest in. Window frame pieces make strong walls with a view.

1×2×2 window frame

2×2 plate floor

DELIGHTFUL DESERT ISLAND

Islands are areas of land, big or small, that are completely surrounded by water. To make a desert island like this one, you'll need lots of tan pieces to make the sandy shores. Remember to add shady palm trees. You never know who might turn up for a visit!

Stack gray and brown slopes and bricks for a craggy cave

I thought you said "dessert" island so I brought treats!

If you have blue plates, add water around your island

Small gray slopes are rocks. You could add seashells, too

Palm tree top has four prongs

6×5 swordleaf

Dinosaur tail piece

PERFECT PALM

A special palm tree top with four prongs connects the leaves to the bendy trunk.

COLORFUL CORAL REEF

Ocean reefs are made of tiny animals called corals. Reefs are home to all kinds of sea plants and creatures. Get creative with the pieces in your collection and try to fill almost every stud of your reef base.

Use plant pieces such as vines for seaweed

I hope I don't see a shark!

ROCKY BASE

Stack bricks and plates on a large baseplate to form a rocky seafloor. Make the piles different heights so that the surface looks real.

Pile of plates for a mound of sand

This reef is built on one tan 16×16 baseplate

Ribbed hose pieces topped with LEGO® Technic balls become underwater plants

BUILD TIP!

Pieces with clips are handy for holding sea creatures such as fish so that it looks like they are swimming.

Groups of transparent flame pieces look like coral

Even a banana piece can become a sea creature!

SANDY SEABED

Plants grow and creatures thrive even at the bottom of the sea! Make a sandy seabed for bottom-dwelling wildlife. Stack up bricks and slopes to make rocky outcrops for sea plants to grow on.

BUILD TIP!

Add a bar with a stud for visiting minifigures to rest on while they observe the seabed.

This starfish connects to a stud of the "rocky" brick

Slope bricks look like rocks on the seafloor

1×1 rock jewel makes a surprising undersea flower

SHOOT UP

Try combining different plant pieces to make sure your seabed is home to a variety of heights and types of plants.

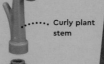

Curly plant stem

1×1 round brick with leaves

ROCKY CAVE

A cave is a rocky hole that can extend deep underground. This one is made from a variety of gray panels, slopes, and bricks, which make its three walls. At the back there is an opening so minifigure explorers can go spelunking.

The smooth side wall is a 1×6×5 panel

Add in different shades for a more natural look

Surround the cave with small stones made from 1×1 slopes

This cave rocks!

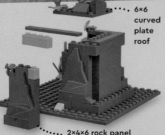

6×6 curved plate roof

ROCK WALL

One of this cave's walls is made of two 2×4×6 rock panels. Build walls on only three sides so there is an opening.

2×4×6 rock panel

BRICK TYPES

When you're planning your nature models, it can be helpful to know which LEGO® pieces you have and what they are called. These are just some of the many LEGO parts you may come across. If you don't have all of these pieces, don't worry! You can make lots of impressive models with the elements you do have.

What brick will I pick?

⚠ Small parts and small balls can cause choking if swallowed. Not for children under 3 years.

MEASUREMENTS

The size of a LEGO piece is described by the number of studs it has. A brick that has two studs along and three studs up is called a 2×3 brick. Tall parts have a third number, which is the height of the piece in standard bricks.

2×3 brick top view

2×3 brick side view

1×1×3 brick side view

BRICKS

Bricks are the basis of most builds. They come in many shapes, sizes, and colors.

2×2 brick

2×2 round brick

1×2 brick

PLATES

Plates have studs on top and tubes on the bottom, but plates are thinner than bricks. Three stacked plates are the same height as one standard brick.

3 stacked 1×2 plates next to a 1×2 brick

2×3 plate

1×1 plate

JUMPER PLATES

These plates have just one stud in the middle, and they let you "jump" the usual grid of LEGO studs. These pieces are useful for centering things in your models.

2×2 jumper plate

1×2 jumper plate

TILES

Tiles have tubes on the bottom and no studs on top. These parts give your builds a smooth finish and printed tiles add more detail.

2×2 tile

Printed eye tile

SIDE STUDS

Pieces with studs on more than one side let you build upward as well as outward.

1×1 brick with side stud

1×2/2×2 bracket

CLIPS

Pieces with clips can attach to other elements, such as bars.

1×2 plate with two clips

1×1 plate with clip

LEGO® TECHNIC

These elements expand the range of functions you can build into your models. They are particularly useful for builds with lots of moving parts or technical details.

1×2 brick with axle hole

LEGO® Technic axle

JOINTS

Add flexibility to your build with parts that have tow balls and sockets.

1×2 plate with ball socket

1×2 plate with tow ball

SLOPES

Slope bricks have diagonal angles. They can be curved or inverted (upside down).

1×1 slope

2×1 inverted slope

3×1 curved slope

HINGES

Add movement to your builds with hinge pieces. Hinge plates and hinge bricks let parts of your builds move from side to side or tilt up and down.

1×2 hinge brick with 2×2 hinge plate (side view)

1×2 hinge brick with 2×2 hinge plate (top view)

DK | Penguin Random House

Senior Editor Tori Kosara
Designer James McKeag
Production Editor Siu Yin Chan
Senior Production Controller Lloyd Robertson
Managing Editor Paula Regan
Managing Art Editor Jo Connor
Publishing Director Mark Searle

Inspirational models built by
Jason Briscoe, Emily Corl, Nate Dias, Yvonne Doyle, Jessica Farrell,
Alice Finch, Rod Gillies, Tim Goddard, Kevin Hall, Tim Johnson,
Barney Main, Simon Pickard, Pete Reid, and Iain Scott

Photography by Gary Ombler
Designed for DK by Thelma-Jane Robb

Dorling Kindersley would like to thank:
Randi Sørensen, Heidi K. Jensen, Lydia Barram, Ashley Blais, Paul Hansford,
Martin Leighton Lindhart, Martin Klingenberg, Nina Koopman, and the LEGO
City Design Team, at the LEGO Group; Julia March for proofreading; Isabelle
Merry for design assistance; and Lori Hand for Americanizing.

First American Edition, 2023
Published in the United States by DK Publishing
1745 Broadway, 20th Floor, New York, NY 10019

Page design copyright © 2023 Dorling Kindersley Limited
DK, a Division of Penguin Random House LLC
23 24 25 26 27 10 9 8 7 6 5 4 3 2 1
001–333941–Mar/2023

Manufactured by Dorling Kindersley,
One Embassy Gardens, 8 Viaduct Gardens, London SW11 7BW, UK
under license from the LEGO Group.

Contains content previously published in *How to Build LEGO® Dinosaurs* (2022),
LEGO® *Animal Atlas* (2018), LEGO® *Christmas Ideas* (2019), LEGO® *City Build
Your Own Adventure* (2016), LEGO® *City Build Your Own Adventure: Catch the
Crooks* (2020), LEGO® *Epic History* (2020), LEGO® *Halloween Ideas* (2020),
LEGO® *Life Hacks* (2021), LEGO® *Magical Ideas* (2021), LEGO® *Party Ideas* (2022),
LEGO® *Play Book* (2013), LEGO® *Super Nature* (2021),
The LEGO® Ideas Book (2022)

A catalog record for this book
is available from the Library of Congress.
ISBN 978-0-7440-7654-7
Printed and bound in China

For the curious

www.dk.com
www.LEGO.com

MIX
Paper | Supporting
responsible forestry
FSC™ C018179
www.fsc.org

This book was made with Forest
Stewardship Council ™ certified
paper—one small step in DK's
commitment to a sustainable future.
**For more information go to
www.dk.com/our-green-pledge**